Drama for Students, Volume 11

Editor: Elizabeth Thomason.

Contributing Editors: Anne Marie Hacht, Michael L. LaBlanc, Ira Mark Milne, Jennifer Smith.

Managing Editor: Dwayne Hayes.

Research: Victoria B. Cariappa, *Research Manager*. Cheryl Warnock, *Research Specialist*. Tamara Nott, Tracie A. Richardson, *Research Associates*. Nicodemus Ford, Sarah Genik, Timothy Lehnerer, *Research Assistants*.

Permissions: Maria Franklin, *Permissions Manager*. Sarah Tomasek, *Permissions Associate*.

Manufacturing: Mary Beth Trimper, *Manager, Composition and Electronic Prepress*. Evi Seoud, *Assistant Manager, Composition Purchasing and Electronic Prepress*. Stacy Melson, *Buyer*.

Imaging and Multimedia Content Team: Barbara

Yarrow, *Manager*. Randy Bassett, *Imaging Supervisor*. Robert Duncan, Dan Newell, *Imaging Specialists*. Pamela A. Reed, *Imaging Coordinator*. Leitha Etheridge-Sims, Mary Grimes, *Image Catalogers*. Robyn V. Young, *Project Manager*. Dean Dauphinais, *Senior Image Editor*. Kelly A. Quin, *Image Editor*.

Product Design Team: Kenn Zorn, *Product Design Manager*. Pamela A. E. Galbreath, *Senior Art Director*. Michael Logusz, *Graphic Artist*.

Copyright Notice

of this work have added value to the underlying factual material herein through one or more of the following: unique and original selection, coordination, expression, arrangement, and classification of the information. All rights to this publication will be vigorously defended.

Copyright © 2001
Gale Group, Inc.
27500 Drake Road
Farmington Hills, MI 48331-3535

ISBN 0-7876-4085-9
ISSN 1094-9232

Printed in the United States of America.
10 9 8 7 6 5 4 3 2 1

The Amen Corner

James Baldwin

1968

Introduction

The Amen Corner, the first dramatic play by the now much-celebrated African-American novelist, essayist, and playwright James Baldwin, was written during the 1950s, first performed on the professional stage in 1965, and first published in 1968.

The Amen Corner takes place in two settings: a "corner" church in Harlem and the apartment dwelling of Margaret Anderson, the church pastor, and of her son, David, and sister Odessa. After giving a fiery Sunday morning sermon, Margaret is confronted by the unexpected arrival of her long estranged husband, Luke, who collapses from illness shortly thereafter. Their son, David, along with several elders of the congregation, learn from Luke that, while Margaret had led everyone to believe that he had abandoned her with their son years ago, it was in fact Margaret who had left Luke in pursuit of a purely religious life. This information precipitates confrontations between Margaret and her son, her congregation, and her estranged husband, regarding what they see as the hypocritical nature of her religious convictions, which she uses to justify the breakup of her family. After an important conversation with his dying father, David informs Margaret that he is leaving home to pursue his calling as a jazz musician. On his deathbed, Luke declares to Margaret that he has always loved her, and that she should not have left him. Finally, Margaret's congregation decides to oust her, based on their perception that she unjustly ruined her own family in the name of religion. Only after losing her son, her husband, and her congregation, does Margaret finally realize that she should not have used religion as an excuse to escape the struggles of life and love, but that "To love the Lord is to love all His children—all of them, everyone!—and suffer with them and rejoice with them and never count the cost!"

The Amen Corner addresses themes of the role of the church in the African-American family, the complex relationship between religion and earthly love, and the effect of a poverty born of racial prejudice on the African-American community.

Themes:
- role of church in the african american family
- relationship between religion and love
- effect of a poverty born of racial prejudice on the african american community

Author Biography

James Baldwin was born on August 2, 1924, in New York City, to David Baldwin, a factory worker and clergyman, and Emma (Jones) Baldwin. Baldwin was the eldest of nine children, whom he spent much of his childhood helping to raise and care for amidst the poverty of black Harlem. During his high school years, the young Baldwin became a revivalist minister for the Fireside Pentecostal Assembly. He graduated from De Witt Clinton High School in 1942, after which he began working in the defense industry in New Jersey. In 1942, when his stepfather died, Baldwin decided to become a writer and moved to Greenwich Village, New York, to pursue his goal. There he took on various unskilled odd jobs while working on his first novel. In 1944, he met the celebrated black novelist Richard Wright, who aided Baldwin's career by helping him to get an Eugene F. Saxton Fellowship. Finding the racism in the United States more and more unbearable, Baldwin in 1948 moved to Paris, where he gained experience and insight crucial to his writing career, his sense of racial heritage, and his sexual identity.

It was during this period that his first two novels, *Go Tell It on the Mountain*(1953) and *Giovanni's Room*(1956), were published. Returning to the United States in 1957, Baldwin became an important public speaker and activist in the burgeoning civil rights movement, a political role he maintained throughout his life. He continued to be a world traveler, living for various periods in France and other countries, as well as in the Untied States. Baldwin wrote distinguished works in several forms. Important essays on racial issues are collected in *Notes of a Native Son*(1955), *Nobody Knows My Name: More Notes of a Native Son*(1961), and *The Fire Next Time*(1963). Notable fiction, besides his first novels, includes *Another Country*(1962) and *If Beale Street Could Talk*(1974). *The Amen Corner*(1955) and *Blues for Mr. Charlie*(1964) are his most celebrated dramas. Baldwin died of stomach cancer on November 30 or December 1 (sources vary), 1987, in St. Paul de Vence, France.

Plot Summary

Act I

Act I takes place "on a Sunday morning in Harlem." It begins with a church service, led by Margaret Anderson, the pastor of a "corner" church. The singing of hymns, accompanied by Margaret's eighteen-year-old son, David, on the piano, is an important element of the service. At one point, Mrs. Ida Jackson, a young woman, walks up to the pulpit holding her sick baby; she asks Margaret what she should do to save her baby, and Margaret advises her to leave her husband, but Mrs. Jackson asserts that she doesn't want to leave her husband.

After the service, Margaret, her sister Odessa, David, and three elders of the church, Sister Moore, Sister Boxer, and Brother Boxer, congregate in Margaret's apartment, which is attached to the church. Margaret's long estranged husband, Luke, arrives unexpectedly at the apartment. In front of David and the church elders, Luke confronts Margaret with the fact that, while she had led everyone to believe that he had abandoned her with their son years earlier, it was in fact Margaret who had left Luke. After an infant of theirs had died, Margaret had blamed Luke for the tragedy, and had abandoned him to pursue a purely religious life. Luke then collapses from illness and is taken to lie down on a bed in Margaret's apartment. Although

David and the others plead with Margaret to stay and care for the dying Luke, Margaret leaves for a brief trip to Philadelphia for the purpose of aiding another church.

Act II

Act II is set the following Saturday afternoon. In the first scene, Odessa, Sister Boxer, and Sister Moore sit in the kitchen of the apartment, discussing Sister Margaret's role in the church, given this new information that she had abandoned her own husband. The church elders express some discontent with Margaret's use of the church funds and with her treatment of the congregation, as well as the hypocrisy they perceive in her years of lying about her relationship with her husband. In the next scene, David enters the room where his father, Luke, lies ill. David and Luke discuss David's ambitions to become a jazz musician and his father's life as a jazz musician. Luke explains to David that being abandoned by Margaret had ruined his life. Luke encourages David to pursue jazz, but also explains to him that music is nothing if a man doesn't have the love of a woman in his life.

During the next scene, in the church, several of the church elders and other congregation members gather to discuss Margaret's position as pastor of the church. They criticize Margaret for her use of church funds, her treatment of her husband, and her seeming hypocrisies in regard to what she preaches versus how she lives her own life. They all break

· use of church funds
· treatment of her husband
· hypocrisy preach x her life

into a hymn, during which Margaret enters the church, just back from Philadelphia. She explains that the Philadelphia congregation will be coming to join their service the next day. They all sing a hymn and then say a prayer.

In the following scene, David brings a record player into the room where Luke lies and plays a record of Luke playing the trombone. Margaret enters the bedroom, and David leaves with the record player. Margaret and Luke then have a conversation about their relationship and the role of religion in Margaret's life, but the two come to no understanding. Odessa then enters and warns Margaret that the church is about to have a business meeting in which they will be discussing Margaret's position as pastor.

Act III

Act III takes place the following Sunday morning. In the first scene, Margaret and Mrs. Jackson talk in the church; Mrs. Jackson's baby has died, but she resists Margaret's religious advice about the matter and insists that she is more concerned with her husband than with religion. In the kitchen of the apartment, Margaret and her sister Odessa discuss Margaret's relationship with Luke. Later in the church, Odessa joins the church elders, who are again discussing their plans to oust Margaret from her post as pastor. Odessa attempts to defend Margaret against this decision. In the apartment, David confronts Margaret with the fact that he has decided to leave home to pursue his calling as a jazz musician.

Margaret enters the bedroom where Luke lies dying, and they discuss David's decision to leave. Margaret and Luke finally make peace with one another and admit that they still love each other; as they embrace, Luke dies. Margaret then enters the church and speaks to the congregation, although she knows that they have chosen to oust her from her position. Margaret tells the congregation that she is "just now finding out what it means to love the Lord." She concludes that "To love the Lord is to love all His children—all of them, everyone!—and suffer with them and rejoice with them and never count the cost!" The congregation breaks into a hymn as Margaret steps down from the pulpit, enters the room where Luke lies dead, and falls beside his body on the bed.

Characters

David Alexander

David is the eighteen-year-old son of Margaret and Luke. David plays the piano in the church during Margaret's sermons, and his mother wants him to pursue a life of devotion to religion, utilizing his musical talents for that purpose only. David, however, has enrolled in a music school, and has been secretly sneaking out to jazz clubs and playing in a jazz band. One night, he sneaks out to hear his estranged father, Luke, also a musician, play at a jazz club. When Luke arrives at Margaret's house, David learns that it was his mother who had left his father, and not his father who had abandoned them, as she had led him to believe. While Margaret had wanted David to accompany her to Philadelphia, David chooses to stay home with his dying father. David and Luke have an important discussion about the family history, his parents' relationship, and jazz music. When Margaret returns from Philadelphia, David confronts her with the decision that he is leaving home to pursue a career as a jazz musician. David tries to explain to his mother that he can make a better contribution to the world through pursuing his own musical calling, pleading with her that "Maybe I can say something—one day—maybe I can say something in music that's never been said before."

Luke Alexander

Luke is the estranged husband of Margaret, and the father of David. Luke arrives unexpectedly at Margaret's house and collapses from illness. He confronts Margaret with the fact that she had left him after blaming him for the death of their infant child years earlier. Margaret is unsympathetic to his pleas of love for her, and leaves for a brief trip to Philadelphia, despite the fact that he lies dying in a bed in her home. While Margaret is gone, Luke has an important conversation with their son, David, in which he tries to explain to David his perspective on his relationship with Margaret. After Margaret returns from Philadelphia, Luke again confronts her with the fact that she had unfairly blamed him for the death of their infant and had used religion as an escape and an excuse to leave him. He tells her that David's decision to leave is a decision to "live," not a moral lapse on his part. Most of all, Luke pleads with Margaret that he loved her and needed her and that she should never have left him. Luke then dies, after which Margaret finally realizes the truth of what he has said.

Margaret Alexander

Margaret Alexander is the pastor of a church. In the first scene of the play, she gives a sermon. She then prepares to leave for a brief trip to Philadelphia to aid another church. As she is about to leave, her estranged husband, Luke, arrives unexpectedly and collapses from illness. Several members of Margaret's congregation learn that while she had lead everyone to believe that Luke had abandoned her with their son, David, in fact it was Margaret who left Luke. Despite the fact that Luke lies on his deathbed in her home, Margaret leaves for Philadelphia anyway. While she is gone, members of her congregation meet to discuss their various dissatisfactions with Margaret's position as pastor of their church. They question her use of church funds as well as the new information that she had abandoned her own husband. When Margaret returns, she is confronted by her son, her estranged husband, and her congregation. David informs her that he has been secretly playing in a jazz band and is going to leave home to pursue a career as a jazz musician. Luke confronts her with the fact that she had blamed him for the death of their infant child years ago and had abandoned him in the name of the service of God; Luke points out Margaret's hypocrisy in using religion as an excuse to escape life. Finally, Margaret's congregation confronts her on similar grounds. Having lost her son, her husband, and her congregation, Margaret finally realizes that religion should not have been an excuse for her to break up her family but a reason for her to stand by her man.

Brother Boxer

Brother Boxer is an elder of Margaret's church who resents her for insisting that it is sinful of him to take a job driving a liquor delivery truck.

Sister Boxer

Sister Boxer is an elder of Margaret's church who criticizes Margaret for insisting that it is sinful for her husband, Brother Boxer, to take a job driving a liquor delivery truck.

Ida Jackson

Ida Jackson is a young woman who steps up to the pulpit during Margaret's sermon with a plea for help for her sick baby. Margaret advises her to leave her husband, but Mrs. Jackson protests that she doesn't want to leave her husband. Later, Mrs. Jackson returns to Margaret for consolation after her baby has died. Again, Mrs. Jackson protests Margaret's religious explanations and consolations, asserting instead that "I just want my man and my home and my children." Margaret tells her that she needs to pray, but Mrs. Jackson disagrees, maintaining that she is going home to her husband instead. Margaret finally realizes that Mrs. Jackson is right to stand by her man, rather than abandon him in the name of religion, telling her, "Get on home to your husband. Go on home, to your man."

Sister Moore

Sister Moore is an elder of Margaret's church who is instrumental in having Margaret ousted from her position as pastor.

Odessa

Odessa is Margaret's sister, who lives with Margaret and David. Odessa is supportive of Margaret, and defends her against the criticism of the members of her congregation.

Themes

Religion

Religion is a central theme in Baldwin's play. The first seventeen pages of the play are taken up with a Sunday morning church sermon, led by the pastor, Sister Margaret Anderson. Baldwin has noted that this material was in part based on his own experiences as a young minister. Baldwin also wished the theater audience to be swept up in the experience of actually attending a church service. The role of religion in Margaret's life is examined and questioned by various characters throughout the play. While Margaret presents herself as a pure, holy woman who has been abandoned by her husband, others point out that she has used religion as an excuse to escape from the problems of the material world. It is Luke who finally impresses upon Margaret the idea that she has misinterpreted the significance of religion. Luke points out that human love is not at odds with religion, but is in fact an important element of religion. It is only after she has lost her son, her husband, and her congregation that Margaret is able to appreciate Luke's words. Her final words to her congregation confirm her understanding.

Poverty

Although not one of the play's most prominent

themes, the impact of poverty permeates the play as an underlying condition of the lives of the characters. Margaret berates Brother Boxer for taking a job driving a liquor delivery truck, asserting that it is sinful of him to spend his day providing liquor to people. Sister Boxer, Brother Boxer's wife, however, complains that Margaret is not taking into account the importance of earning a living and supporting a family. In other words, it is economic necessity, based on the limited availability of jobs to African-American men during that time period, which requires that Brother Boxer accept the best job he can find. Poverty is also an underlying theme in the death of Margaret's infant, years before the play takes place, and the death of Mrs. Ida Jackson's infant. It is made clear that these babies became sick and died due to poor nutrition (and perhaps inadequate medical care) because of their poverty. Reference is also made to the limited availability of jobs for African-American women, as one character refers to her work as a maid in the home of a white woman. Thus, while there are no white characters who appear in the play, the black community is presented within a broader context of racial inequality in which African-American women have little choice but to work in positions of servitude to white women, and African-American men are compelled to accept whatever jobs may be available to them.

Love

Many critics have noted that one of the

recurring themes throughout Baldwin's fiction is that of love. Baldwin states in his "Notes" to the published play that the first line he wrote was Margaret's in Act III: "It's an awful thing to think about, the way love never dies!" Margaret throughout most of the play has made the mistake of substituting religion for the love of her own husband. Luke insists that he still loves her, and yet she continues to deny her own feelings of love for him. Through the character of Luke, the love of a woman is presented as a necessity to the survival of black men in a racist society; Luke's downfall is attributed to Margaret's withholding of love from him. It is only at the end, just before Luke dies, that Margaret is able to understand the power of love: "Maybe it's not possible to stop loving anybody you ever really loved. I never stopped loving you, Luke. I tried. But I never stopped loving you." Baldwin explains that although Margaret, by the end, "has lost everything," she "also gains the keys to the kingdom." He goes on to say that "The kingdom is love, and love is selfless, although only the self can lead one there. She gains herself."

Topics for Further Study

- In addition to plays and novels, Baldwin has been celebrated for his essays on issues of race in America. Read one of Baldwin's essays, such as from his collections: *Notes from a Native Son*(1955), *Nobody Knows My Name*(1961), or *The Fire Next Time*(1963). What are some of Baldwin's central concerns with the issue of race in America? What solutions does he suggest for addressing issues of racial inequality? In what ways are these concerns addressed in his play *The Amen Corner*?

- Pick a particularly moving or important scene from *The Amen Corner* to perform with another student (or students). How does performing a scene from the play help you to understand the motivations of certain characters or to illuminate key thematic concerns of the play? In what ways could different performance choices affect the meaning, effect, or impact of that particular scene?

- Baldwin's play addresses issues of race and poverty in terms of the significance of the black church to an African-American family. Learn more about the role of the church in the history of African-American culture and the struggles of African Americans for racial equality in America. In what ways has religion and the institution of the church been an important factor in African-American history and African-American communities?

- Baldwin's play focuses on the role of the wife and mother in an African-American family. Another important and much celebrated African-American playwright who addresses the role of African-American women in the black family is Ntozake Shange, who is best known for her play *for colored girls who have considered suicide when the rainbow is enuf.* Learn more about this playwright and her works. In what ways does she address similar issues to those addressed by Baldwin in his play? In what ways does she provide a different perspective on male-female relationships in the African-American community?

Staging

Baldwin wrote this play with a very specific stage set in mind. The two main parts of the set are the church and the adjoining apartment. The positioning of the church in relation to the apartment is symbolic of the role of the church in the life of the family. The stage notes indicate that "The church is on a level above the apartment and should give the impression of dominating the family's living quarters." This is meant to symbolize the dominating influence of the church on Margaret's family. The set design within the church is also a key element of Baldwin's vision for this play. The stage notes indicate that the church "is dominated by the pulpit, on a platform, upstage." Thus, within the church itself, Margaret, as the pastor giving sermons, is the dominant figure. This set design emphasizes the extent to which the church is an arena in which Margaret holds a great deal of power, as opposed to the rest of the world, in which she is an impoverished single black woman. The program notes also mention that on the platform on which the pulpit sits is "a thronelike chair." The implication is that, in the world of her congregation, Margaret reigns supreme, as if she were royalty. This again emphasizes, by way of contrast, the extent to which, in the rest of the world, Margaret as a poor African-American woman is virtually powerless. Finally, Baldwin wanted the stage set of the church to position the audience of the play itself as if they, too, were members of the congregation, listening to Margaret's sermons. This positioning of the audience is key to one of Baldwin's central goals in writing this play: to suggest a parallel between theatrical elements of performance and audience participation in the black church with that of the theater.

Sermons

A central element of Baldwin's play is the church sermons led by Pastor Margaret. As he has stated in his "Notes" which preface the published edition of the play: "I knew that out of the ritual of the church, historically speaking, comes the act of the theatre, the communion which is the theatre. And I knew that what I wanted to do in the theatre was to recreate moments I remembered, as a boy preacher, to involve the people, even against their will, to shake them up, and, hopefully, to change them." The long service that begins the play alternates the singing of hymns with a fiery sermon by Sister Margaret. Margaret's sermon is written in the highly developed and stylized oratory style of African-American ministers. This oratory style is most easily recognized by the use of repetition of key phrases and the use of black English vernacular. The civil rights activist Reverend Martin Luther King, Jr. has been widely noted for his skill and mastery of this oratory style, particularly as exemplified by his famous "I Have a Dream" speech.

African-American Literary Movements

Twentieth-century African-American literature has been characterized by two important literary movements: the Harlem Renaissance and the Black Arts Movement. The Harlem Renaissance, also referred to as the New Negro Movement, designates a period during the 1920s in which African-American literature flourished among a group of writers concentrated in the Harlem section of New York City. Important writers of the Harlem Renaissance include James Weldon Johnson, who wrote the novel *Autobiography of an Ex-Colored Man*(1912); Claude McKay, who wrote the bestselling novel *Home to Harlem*(1928); Langston Hughes, who wrote the poetry collection *The Weary Blues*(1926); and Wallace Thurman, who wrote the novel *The Blacker the Berry*(1929). This period of incredible literary output diminished when the Great Depression of the 1930s affected the financial status of many African-American writers. The Black Arts Movement, also referred to as the Black Aesthetic Movement flourished during the 1960s and 70s, and embodied values derived from black nationalism and promoted politically and socially significant works, often written in Black English vernacular. Important writers of the Black Arts Movement include Imamu Amiri Baraka (also known as LeRoi Jones), Eldridge Cleaver, Angela Davis, Alice Walker, and Toni Morrison.

Black Theater

Dramatic works by African-American writers in the nineteenth century include *King Shotaway*(1823), by William Henry Brown, the first known play by an African-American writer; *The Escape: or, A Leap for Freedom*(1858), by William Wells Brown, the first play by an African-American writer to be published; and *Rachel*(1916), by Anglina W. Grimke, the first successful stage play by an African-American writer. Important literary movements, such as the Harlem Renaissance and the Black Arts Movement, influenced dramatic works and stage productions by African Americans in the twentieth century. The development of Black Theater in the first half of the twentieth century was inspired by the Harlem Renaissance, and included the establishment of theaters devoted to black productions in major cities throughout the United States. The most prominent black theaters by mid-century were the American Negro Theater and the Negro Playwrights' Company. In the post-World War II era, black theater became more overtly political and more specifically focused on celebrating African-American culture. One of the most prominent works to emerge from this period was the 1959 play, *A Raisin in the Sun,* by Lorraine Hansberry. The Black Arts Movement, which emerged in the 1960s, led to the establishment in

1965 of the Repertory Theater of Harlem, initiated by Amiri Baraka (still LeRoi Jones at that time). Baraka's award-winning 1964 play, *The Dutchman,* is among the most celebrated dramatic works of this period. Ntozake Shange's 1977, *for colored girls who have considered suicide, when the rainbow is enuf,* utilized an experimental dramatic format to address issues facing African-American women. In the 1980s, August Wilson emerged as an important African-American playwright with his *Ma Rainey's Black Bottom*(1985), about a blues singer and her band, set in Chicago in the 1920s.

Critical Overview

In his "Notes" for the first publication of *The Amen Corner* in 1968, Baldwin recalls that writing the play was "a desperate and even rather irresponsible act." With one published novel to his name *(Go Tell It on the Mountain),* Baldwin was not in a strong position to succeed with his first play. As his agent at the time informed him, "the American theatre was not exactly clamoring for plays on obscure aspects of Negro life, especially one written by a virtually unknown author whose principal effort until that time had been one novel." Nevertheless, Baldwin forged ahead, and *The Amen Corner,* written in the 1950s, was first produced on the campus of Howard University, then in Los Angeles, before opening on Broadway in 1965. While it won the 1964 Foreign Drama Critics Circle Award, the play was not published in book form until 1968.

Compare & Contrast

- **1920s:** The Harlem Renaissance characterizes a period of flowering of African-American literature.

- **1960s:** The Black Arts Movement, also called the Black Aesthetic Movement, inspired in part by the Civil Rights Movement, represents the cutting edge of African-

American artistic and literary style and philosophy.

- **1990s:** A new generation of African-American writers and artists have been greatly influenced by the legacy of the Black Arts Movement.

- **1950s:** The most prominent Black theaters in the United States include the American Negro Theater and the Negro Playwrights' Company.

  1960s: Inspired by, and in part an initiator of, the Black Arts Movement, Amiri Baraka establishes the Black Repertory Theater in Harlem.

  1990s: Numerous black theaters have been established throughout the United States, with many mainstream stages also featuring black theatrical productions.

- **1954:** In the decision of *Brown* vs. *the Board of Education,* the Supreme Court declares that racially segregated schools are unconstitutional. This initiates the desegregation of public schools in the United States.

  1955: Rosa Parks initiates the Montgomery bus boycott in protest against seating segregation on public buses.

1961: Over 70,000 college students, in what are called "Freedom Rides," travel to the South to register black voters.

1964: An extensive Civil Rights Act is passed by Congress, declaring various forms of racial discrimination illegal.

1965: The Voting Rights Act is passed to protect African Americans against discriminatory tactics in regard to voting.

- **1963:** President John F. Kennedy is assassinated.

1964: Martin Luther King, Jr., is awarded the Nobel Peace Prize for his achievements in the Civil Rights Movement.

1965: Black Muslim leader Malcolm X, who promoted Black Nationalism, is assassinated.

1966: The Black Panther Party, a revolutionary organization of African Americans, is founded by Huey Newton and Bobby Seale.

1968: Martin Luther King, Jr., is assassinated.

1980s: The Black Panther party is essentially disbanded.

Critics have commented on the artistic success of Baldwin's play as a dramatic stage production. Carlton W. Molette, writing in 1977, stated that *The Amen Corner* "is one of the most successful Afro-American plays that I have seen." Molette asserts that "The first professional production was moving as theater ought to be but seldom is." Carolyn Wedin Sylvander, asserting that *"The Amen Corner* is a better play than its production history or critical attention would seem to indicate," especially praises the play for its qualities as a stage production, particularly in Baldwin's use of music: "the play is certainly constructed in such a way as to truly 'come alive' on the stage. Much of that liveliness and power to involve is transmitted through the music. Group singing, individual singing, instrumental accompaniment, jazz (Luke on record), all provide choral commentary on character and conflict."

Several critics have noted the play's embodiment of aesthetic values put forth by the Black Arts Movement of the 1960s. Darwin T. Turner explains that *"The Amen Corner* seems more clearly designed as a drama written about black experience for a black audience. In this respect, it resembles Black Arts drama, in which the dramatist presumes that he must write without concern for the white spectator, who exists outside the black experience and without comprehension of it. I do not wish to imply that Baldwin consciously designed the play for the education of a black audience. Instead, I am suggesting that he found strength in writing meaningfully about an experience he knew while assuming that his audience would be equally familiar with that experience." Turner concludes that Baldwin's "success, I feel, did not result solely from his recreation of a church setting that was familiar to him but from his presumption that his audience required no interpretation, no modification, because it already knew the cultural setting. Thus Baldwin achieved an artistic freedom rarely granted a black dramatist except when he works within the theater of a black community." Molette provides a similar assessment of Baldwin's play in terms of the ways in which it addresses its audience: *The Amen Corner* does not protest to whites; it informs, educates, illuminates blacks.... It is not self-consciously black. The play assumes that there are some elementary aspects of black culture that do not require explanation within the body of the play. It assumes, in effect, a black audience. It is not an anti-white play, it is an a-white play."

Molette, however, does note that "the play is not perfect," pointing out that "Ironically, *The Amen Corner* is at its worst as a play precisely when it is at its best as literature. There are several two-character scenes between the members of the Alexander family that are true literary gems. They are also the scenes of greatest character revelation. They actually tell us too much about the characters. Now, all that is told needs to be told; but some of it ought to be told through means other than words." Molette goes on to criticize scenes that are particularly static and lacking in drama when seen on stage.

For example, in Act II,"the action slows down, and the words become far more important than the deed. In the theater, that usually means trouble. This is especially a problem with the scenes that involve the father (Luke), because he is confined to his sickbed, making visual interest through movement very difficult to achieve, as well."

Fred L. Standley praises the play, along with other works by Baldwin, for his treatment of "a variety of thematic concerns: the historical significance and the potential explosiveness in black-white relations; the necessity for developing a sexual and psychological consciousness and identity; the intertwining of love and power in the universal scheme of existence as well as in the structures of society; the misplaced priorities in the value systems in America; and the responsibility of the artist to promote the evolution of the individual and the society."

Trudier Harris criticized Baldwin's portrayal of female characters in a number of his works, asserting that "Few women in Baldwin's works are able to move beyond the bounds of the traditional roles that have been cut out for them and in which the use of their bodies is the most important factor." Harris offers both criticism and praise, however, of Baldwin's representation of women through the character of Margaret in *The Amen Corner*. She states that Sister Margaret "is most like the women in the fiction in her desire and ability to serve.... In her adherence to scripture, she is one of the most fanatical of Baldwin's black women characters. Yet in her recognition of the unrelenting antagonism between males and females, she voices the plight of all of the church-based women." Harris concludes, however, that, in Baldwin's fiction and drama, "for all this growth and progression, for all this freedom of action and movement, the women are still confined to niches carved out for them by men whose egos are too fragile to grant their equality."

What Do I Read Next?

- *Blues for Mr. Charlie*(1964), Baldwin's most noted play, was performed on Broadway in 1964 and received a Foreign Drama Critics Award. "Mr. Charlie" is a name used to refer to the white man.

- *Notes of a Native Son*(1955) is Baldwin's first collection of essays on issues of race in America.

- *Nobody Knows My Name: More Notes of a Native Son*(1961) is Baldwin's second collection of essays on racial relations in America.

- *The Fire Next Time*(1963) is an essay by Baldwin based on an article published in the *New Yorker* magazine in 1962, and addresses issues of racial relations in America.

- *Go Tell It on the Mountain*(1953) is Baldwin's first novel and the work for which he is best known and most celebrated. It is an autobiographical account of Baldwin's childhood and early religious influences.

- *Giovanni's Room*(1977) is Baldwin's second novel and concerns a young man in Paris struggling with his sexual identity.

- *Native Son*(1955) is a novel by the celebrated African-American writer Richard Wright, who was an important role model for Baldwin and important early influence on his writing career.

Sources

Baldwin, James, "Notes" to *The Amen Corner,* Dial Press, 1968, pp. xv-xvi.

Harris, Trudier, *Black Women in the Fiction of James Baldwin,* University of Tennessee Press, 1985, pp. 9-11.

Molette, Carlton W., "James Baldwin as Playwright," in *James Baldwin: A Critical Evaluation,* edited by Therman B. O'Daniel, Howard University Press, 1977, pp. 184-86.

Standley, Fred. L., "James Baldwin as Dramatist," in *Critical Essays on James Baldwin,* edited by Fred L. Standley and Nancy V. Burt, G. K. Hall, 1977, p. 302.

Sylvander, Carolyn Wedin, *James Baldwin,* Frederick Ungar Publishing Co., 1980, pp. 91, 96.

Turner, Darwin T., "James Baldwin and the Dilemma of the Black Dramatist," in *James Baldwin: A Critical Evaluation,* edited by Therman B. O'Daniel, Howard University Press, pp. 192, 194.

Further Reading

Baraka, Amiri (LeRoi Jones), *The Dutchman and the Slave Ship: Two Plays,* Morrow, 1964.

> These two plays are critically acclaimed pieces by one of the leading writers of the Blacks Arts Movement.

Harris, Trudier, *Black Women in the Fiction of James Baldwin,* University of Tennessee Press, 1985.

> This book is a critical assessment of the female characters in Baldwin's fiction.

Jones, LeRoi (Imamu Amiri Baraka) and Larry Neal, eds., *Black Fire: An Anthology of African-American Writing,* Morrow, 1968.

> This text is an important collection of works emanating from the Black Arts Movement of the 1960s and 70s.

Leeming, David Adams, *James Baldwin: A Biography,* Knopf, 1994.

> Leeming's book is a recent and highly enjoyable biography of Baldwin.

Shange, Ntozake, *for colored girls who have considered suicide, when the rainbow is enuf: A*

Choreopoem, Scribner Poetry, 1997.

> Shange's play is an important experimental dramatic work (first published in 1977) that emerged from the Black Arts Movement. It addresses issues of African-American women in terms of racism and sexism.

CPSIA information can be obtained
at www.ICGtesting.com
Printed in the USA
LVHW021254080921
697311LV00011B/797